Something for Everyone

People's poetry and prose taken from the columns of City Press over a period of ten years (1982–1992)

Editor:
QEDUSIZI BUTHELEZI

Via Afrika Limited, Reg. No. 70/03235/06
1064 Arcadia Street, Hatfield
P.O. Box 151, Pretoria 0001
Cover design and typography by Via Afrika Limited
Set in 11 on 12 Palatino
by A1 Graphics, Pretoria
Lithographed and bound by National Book Printers
Goodwood

ISBN 0 7994 1328 3

First Edition
First Impression – December 1992

Dedication

This book is dedicated to all the young people of South Africa, especially those who voiced their feelings, opinions, fears and aspirations during the turbulent times of 1982 to 1992.

Let us celebrate this decade of fruition through the spirit of merriment as expressed by Simon Masemula when he says:

Oh Shadow, dear shadow
Come, shadow and dance.
On the wall, in the firelight
Let both of us prance
I raise my arms thus!
And you raise yours
And dancing, leaping
And laughing we go.
From the wall to the ceiling
From the ceiling to the wall.

Foreword

It is often said that a successful newspaper is judged by the readers' letters to the Editor.

City Press is no exception to the rule.

However, we realised that the letters page alone could not accommodate the range of topics and volume of letters submitted. Frequently many worthwhile letters do not see the light of day.

Also, the selection of letters is normally left to the discretion of the Editor. This constraint frustrates many readers, especially the youth in our country, who need a forum for expression.

South Africa is in a turbulent state – borne out of the years of oppression and suppression of ideas and free speech. To remove this lid in order to create freedom of expression, we started a forum in City Press called Kiddies' Corner.

Through the years countless numbers of our youth sent their contributions – poems, short stories, jokes, drawings etc. to Kiddies' Corner.

Our youth also lived through some of the phases that our country went through. They have experienced incidents around them. Impressions were also embedded in their minds – some with hate, some with hope and some with humour.

The purpose of this book, therefore, is to depict the country we live in through the eyes of our youth – how they see the violence that has gripped their community. The bloodletting that has pitted brother against brother, the frustration caused by unemployment and re-trenchments, the return of exiles and the daily frustrations caused by attacks on commuters.

Through this exercise of uncensored expression by our youth, we have been able to highlight the feelings they experience and, in some cases, have contributed to solving these problems.

We see Kiddies' Corner as an investment in our country's most valuable asset – our children.

It is an honour for City Press to publish this book as we reach another milestone, our tenth anniversary, and to look back at how our youth see the past, the present and the future.

Khulu Sibiya
Editor: City Press

Introduction

To be asked to collate, compile and suggest titles to an anthology of poetry and prose written by young gifted talent, is a daunting task. For one thing, you spend some time agonising over how to select the "cream of the crop" judiciously without discriminating against those who do not enter the final stakes. Moreover, you also want to make sure that you encourage those would-be writers or artists who are lying fallow somewhere, writers or artists who have not yet found a creative outlet such as City Press' "Kiddies' Corner".

This book serves to celebrate the 10th-year anniversary of the existence of City Press. To commemorate this historic event, 77 poems and prose entries, collected over a period of nearly ten years, have been selected from a possible of 250 and eventually compiled into this book. All these entries have therefore appeared in "Kiddies' Corner".

Efforts have been made not to 'censor' the themes, no matter how sensitive they may be. Instead, the themes covered are reflective of the South African scenario over the decade, as seen through the eyes of the youth.

All contributions are presented in their original form. That is to say, the works have not been edited for grammatical or stylistic errors or any of the criteria traditionally used to judge a "work of art". Instead, creativity, innovativeness and the topicality of the subject have been the chief criteria for inclusion.

Congratulations to City Press for their sterling work in providing a literary forum for our youth despite the turbulent ten years of our history. The Family Fun page in general, and the "Kiddies' Corner" in particular, have been a source of inspiration to our youth who more than ever need to be inculcated into both a reading and a writing culture.

Congratulations, too, to the contributors of this volume, some of whom write in a spirit of child-like innocence as the following poem demonstrates:

CITY PRESS, the wonderful newspaper
In South Africa we are proud of you
Today we are what we are because of you
Young and old enjoy reading you
People are proud of you
Reading your paper every Sunday
Enjoying the news that you bring to us
Some are far and some are near
South Africans are proud of you.

– Jerry Seanego, Mabopane.

Qedusizi Buthelezi
Soweto, Johannesburg
30 March 1992

We thank the following young people for their contributions:

Simon Masemula, Jerry Seanego, Dumsani Mbatha, Peter Mahase, Elias Dlamini, Khayaletu Mancotywa, Jeffrey Lepele, Gideon Muthumbe, Johnny Mithani, Robert Nevhulaudzi, Robert Ntombela, Eunah Ndhlovu, Petro Jele, Joseph Nkambule, Sipho Mdluli, Camagu, Nkuhlu, Themba Banda, James Mothapo, Jeffrey Masemene, Sipho Mokoena, Tsholofelo Mosia, Julius Dhlamini, Sibusiso Mnisi, Richard Hlongwane, Abraham Seakamela, Curtis Flame, Martins Sebaka, G O Motsage, Richard Shilenge, George Mokoena, Thekwini Ncongwane, Ronnie Nemungadi, Robert Siele, Leonard Maifala, Reckson Makunga, Carlo Matabane, Harrison Motlhari, Ernest Nyerenda, David Hlatswayo, Gerald Mzizi, Tumelo Leballo, Zakhele Ntshangase, Mkhethwa Shongwe, Mavis Seema, Vincent Temba, Simon Mosolotsane, Benedict Khumalo, Joshua Moroenyane, Zakhele Hadebe, Edwin Mahange, Meshack Madonsela, Tshidiso Motale, Michael Jaca, Benjamin Radebe, Isaac Tshepo, Vusumzi Tshabalala, Irvin Molelekoa, Thabeki Mbele, Ishamael Ngozo, Faith Rabotapi, "Sonto", Albert Ntlonti, Betram Kwenene, Mongesi Nkonzombi, Simphiwe Piliso, David Mashakwe-Tswai.

Contents

Contents

APARTHEID

"SANCTIONS"

NOW

LONDON FLAG

An Anti-Apartheid Demonstration in London in 1987 What is Meant By The Slogan 'Sanctions Now'?

By Edmund "Ma-Khidos" Chitimbe (Mordder-Bee Prison Art.)

Board number 57/0964 "I'm a prisoner" c°Block.

Bloody apartheid, dismantle yourself

Violence is your strongest weapon
Sorrow is your happiness and joy
Separation is the spear you stab your enemy
Apartheid, dismantle yourself

Apartheid where is your sting
How many people have you killed
How many orphans have you created
Does this bring joy to you apartheid
Our jails are full of our innocent brothers
What about our sisters who live in your cells
Apartheid, dismantle yourself now

Apartheid we will not surrender to you
You have kept us voiceless for years in jail
Yet we are fully armed to fight you
Tear down your walls, we will disarm
Our anger has sent us to the bush
We are prepared to fight till you die
Freedom or death, victory is certain
Your creators have died, and your death is
inevitable
Apartheid, dismantle yourself

Apartheid you are worse than
A senseless thing
You have caused black on black violence
Black blood is the water you
Have drunk for years

Black corpses are the meat you
Have eaten for years
We have no more tears
Apartheid, dismantle yourself

Whites love thee not
Blacks love thee not
Indians love thee not
Coloureds love thee not
We want no war
But peace in Africa
Leaders of all your children
Apartheid, dismantle yourself

– Dumsani Mbatha, P.O. Chiawelo.

The twins of apartheid

THE dompas decided my fate
The language I should speak
The school I would attend.

The dompas divorced me from the nation
Demoralised my people
Deprived me of my human rights
Enslaved my mind.

Now the ID I carry
Enhances the power of apartheid
And blindfolds the nation.

The dompas and the ID I carry
Are the twins of apartheid
The roots of violence.

– Peter Mahase, Mokodumela.

Dompas: Colloquialism among Black
people for a reference book

State of Emergency and eviction

People are dying every day
Old and young the same
Father and mother the same
Boys and girls the same
Adults or young ones the same
State of Emergency

The roads have been closed
Only limited movement is allowed
Freedom songs are banned
Freedom clothes are banned
State of Emergency

Time is limited
Funerals are restricted
Five minutes for a funeral
Five minutes to bury you
That's your funeral
They choose their own priest
State of Emergency

What's happened
Who has died?
It's government, soldiers, it's question, reply
It's an oppressed black Africa
We have no place for burial
No place to love
State of Emergency

Today evictions take place
People thrown out with belongings
The shacks are built
In the early morning the shacks are destroyed
Today the shacks are burnt
There is no place to live

Today the squatters and slums Bill
Tomorrow is LTA and Urban Foundation
Only those who have money got houses
State of Emergency

– Mafelefetsane Elias Dlamini, Sebokeng

A miner's plaintive call

ORYSAUSVILLE Mine is my employer
Rock blasting is my speciality
Precious stone is our target.

Deep down to the belly of the earth we are
ferried
Mine lift is our transport to and from
Its speed is tantamount to lightning
When it starts to move
You get a chill running down your spine.

Eerie silence reigns in the lift box
Each "commuter" quietly speaks with his
own God:
"Almighty God, get yourself behind the
wheel …"
"Heavenly Father, I am still too young to die…"
"Lord, I've got six kids whose mother isn't
working."

Reaching our destination safe
is not the end of the game.
"Rockfall" is verse two of our players
Numerous thoughts haunt our minds and
hearts –
"Kinross Mine incident";
"12 people dead in Vaal Reefs Mines
after rockfall … their names have been withheld
until their next of kin have been notified."
"Six Stilfontein miners fitted with artificial legs,
two others confined to wheelchairs after injuries."

But at the end of the day a pittance pays our pains
"the small change of our bosses".
This is painful
This is exploitation
It should not go unchallenged
It dehumanises both the employer and the employee.

– Khayaletu "Shoes" Mancotywa, Thabong (Welkom)

A hope-inspiring dream

I dreamt last night that
there was peace
in South Africa

I dreamt that all people,
black and white
lived as one.

I dreamt there was no
bloodshed and tears.

I dreamt that apartheid
was a thing
of the past.

And then! I woke up!

There is war in South Africa
apartheid is still going strong
and people are not equal.

But there's something I would
like to say to
all those people in the
government.

I am a black child of
South Africa
I was born here and
I will die here
I have a right to be here
No less than the trees and the stars.

And whether or not it is
clear to me
no doubt
South Africa is unfolding as it should
With all its broken dreams.

– Jeffrey "Malefetsane" Lepele,
P O Katlehong.

Not what you know but who

When I apply for a study bursary
My passmark is not what counts
But my surname will be investigated
If it's not right, I am disqualified
I am a victim of nepotism in Venda

When I need a job
My qualification is not important
In the interview they ask
Who do I know in this department?
How am I related to him?
What job is he doing?
If I have no family in top posts
I will not get a job
I am a victim of nepotism in Venda

When I apply for a business site
I will not be considered
What's important is my surname
If it's not the right one
I am disqualified
I am a victim of nepotism in Venda

When I report a crime to the police
Instead of the accused being tried
He is freed because he is of royal blood
I am a victim of nepotism in Venda

– Gideon Muthumbe, Thulaudzi (Venda).

A satire on Bantustans

I am Lennox Sebe, I rule with an iron fist.
There I come, I am Charles Sebe, I attempt a
twist,
I ultimately get a handcuff, on my wrist.
I am Oupa Gxozo, I am sick and tired of the circus.
I have the potential, I put an end to the circus.
Citizens and students jump in joy, Sebe is out
of the track.
If Mangope did it, I can do it as well.
I call myself Venda, I shall show you I will do it.
Up in the north-east of the Transvaal, I shall
celebrate.
I shall tell my people, Vendas, they shall com-
memorate.
They take my work into consideration, they
are dehumanised.
I am Mphephu, the bespectacled "intellectual".
I shall have my own "Radio-Venda" and
Venda Sun.
I shall allow no opposition, my soldiers shall
use coercion.
I shall have plentiful fruit, there shall not be
malnutrition.
But gone are my days, the fruit has perished.
Ravhele is the present Sphinx. He shall follow
suit.
And that is: Going back to where he belongs,
South Africa.

– Johnny Mithani, Bekkersdal Township
(Westonaria).

Bad news for meat thieves

One day two friends went to a butchery to buy meat.

As there was no one to serve them, they stole a parcel of meat.

When they arrived at home they wondered whether the meat was poisoned.

One of then had a solution. "Let's give the dog a piece of meat. If the dog dies we will know there is something wrong."

So they gave the dog a piece of meat.

After 15 minutes they ate the meat.

Later they went to a shebeen.

Soon the younger brother arrived and said the dog had died.

The friends ran outside in panic and forced themselves to vomit up their food. Once they recovered they returned to the boy and said: "Tell us how the dog died."

"It was run over by a car," the boy replied.

– Author unknown.

A shocking mirror

There was once an old woman who lived with her only son. One day her son bought a big mirror which he hung on the wall of the main bedroom.

One day the old woman entered the bedroom, and when she looked at the wall, saw another old woman. She shouted loudly at the other woman.

"Woman, what do you want here inside my son's bedroom?" but got no reply. She then pointed a finger at the old woman, and saw the old woman also pointing a finger at her. She became very angry and said: "Are you also pointing your finger at me? Do you want to fight me? I will show you."

She then took a large stick and went straight to the wall and started beating the image. She smashed the mirror and the pieces fell all over the floor.

When the old woman's son arrived, he said: "Mother, it was not another woman whom you saw, the person you saw was yourself in the mirror".

– Robert Nevhulaudzi, Sibasa (Venda).

No rest for a tired old driver

A tired old driver parked his car on the roadside to take a nap.

After a short while a jogger without a watch came and suddenly stopped to ask for the time. He knocked at the window of the old man's car and said: "Please sir, what is the time?"

The old man wiped his eyes, looked at his watch and said: "It's quarter to six."

"Thank you," said the jogger and passed on his way.

Five minutes later another jogger came and asked the same question as the first jogger. This time the old man got upset and replied: "It's 10 to six, and you people must stop worrying me because I'm having a rest."

Suddenly a good plan flashed into the old man's mind. He wrote a note on a piece of paper which he stuck onto his car window. It stated: "I don't have the time."

He did this to prevent joggers without watches from asking him the time when they are passing by.

Ten minutes later another jogger came by and noticed the piece of paper on the window. Thinking that the man had no watch, the jogger looked at his, knocked at the car window and said: "Hey mister, it's six o'clock."

– Robert M Ntombela, Redhill (Natal).

Teacher fails to explain fully

Once at the WW Stain Primary School, a grade one teacher told the children to bring old things to school. She did not explain to the children what kind of things she wanted. The teacher wanted old tablecloths and old cups.

The next day the principal was shocked when he found many old grandparents in the school yard.

He asked the children: "What are your grandparents doing here?" They replied: "Our class teacher told us to come with old things, so we decided to come with our grandparents."

The principal then said to the grandparents: "Your grandchildren made a mistake – they did not understand their teacher very well."

But the mistake was made by the teacher. She did not explain what kind of old things she wanted.

– Eunah Ndhlovu, P.O. Rethabile.

Honesty not always the best

Uncle Majola worked on a farm in the Transvaal.

There was a bad drought. The grass was dying and the sheep stumbled from one dry patch to another.

Uncle Majola lived in a tiny shack on the farm with his wife and six children.

He was poor but very honest, and honesty is what he taught his children. "Never lie or steal," he always told them.

Uncle Majola's children learnt this lesson so well, even the farmer praised their honesty.

But the drought turned these honest children into very hungry children. Uncle Majola watched sadly as his family went to bed hungry.

Uncle Majola hoped the farmer would give him a sheep to feed his family. But the farmer would not part with even one sheep.

Eventually he could stand it no more. "I am going to steal a sheep tonight," he told his wife.

She gasped! Was this her honest husband talking?

"I have no choice," Majola said. "Our children are starving."

"But they will tell the farmer," she said. "Remember what you have taught them about honesty."

But he had a plan. That night he crept into the sheep pen and grabbed a lamb.

His family feasted for hours. When the

18

children had gone to bed, Uncle Majola carried out his plan.

He connected his hosepipe to the tap and sent water gushing on to his roof for an hour. The next day the farmer noticed a lamb was missing. "It must be Majola," he decided. "But I will catch him out."

So off he went to Uncle Majola's shack. He called the children together and asked them: "When was the last time you ate meat?"

The children remembered the delicious stew they had eaten the night before, but they also remembered the water falling on the roof.

"The last time we ate meat was the night before the big rains came," they said.

– PT Jele, Embalenhle.

Pretoria

A town beautiful and glittering
yet its heart so ugly and dark
Pretoria by name

A town highly respected and honoured
Its soil rich and fertile
yet its people poor and hungry
Pretoria the shame.

A town wonderful and lovable
yet its laws hated and disliked
with its penalties cruel and unfair
Pretoria you're framed

A town so important and famous
yet its record notorious
its atmosphere polluted with tearsmoke and
bullets
Pretoria's not famed

A town clean and cool
yet its spirit evil and cruel
with some buildings huge and tall
and shacks poky and small – Pretoria.

– Joseph Nkambule, Middelburg (Tvl).

Victory is certain

It doesn't matter
How many of us
Have been kept silent
behind bars
Victory is certain

It doesn't matter
How many young lions
They have killed
We will conquer

It doesn't matter
How many laws
They have imposed to
protect apartheid
We will scrap it

It doesn't matter
How many of us
They have penalised
We will fight to victory

It doesn't matter
How hard the forces of
the regime
Try to prevent us
From gaining our freedom
We will get it.

– Sipho Mdluli, Alexandra Township.

Colour-coded

White man, you must be colour-blind;
Or aren't you just being unkind?
You say you are green with envy;
And you turn red when angry.
A coward, you say, is yellow;
You are blue when your spirits are low
Someone gives you black looks,
When you are in their bad books.
You say you are in a brown study,
When, say, you are thinking about your
buddy.
You probably become even more white
When suddenly fraught with fright!
Yet you make my life so hard,
You have the nerve to call me coloured!

– Camagu Nkuhlu, Cofimvaba.

Patience in the face of the struggle

I have been patient enough to experience
the evil of apartheid
I have been patient enough to sit
at the apartheid desk for the enforced
Bantu Education
I have been patient enough to live on the
reserves with no freedom of movement
I have been patient enough to be fed
government propaganda
All this I have done with patience
and goodwill
I have waited for the end of apartheid.

Patiently I have knocked on the
tricameral door
I have been answered with harassment
Patiently I have preached for the end of
apartheid
I have been answered with emergency
regulations
All this I have done with patience and goodwill
I have waited for the end of apartheid.

But I have never heard of the consequences
of my goodwill
I have not reaped the fruit of my kindness
Yes, I have tried to be patient but it
promises no flowers
But the struggle promises victory, struggle

is the coffin in which to put our patience
Struggle is the only grave to bury our
sufferings and poverty.

– Themba Banda, Tembisa.

Raise the black, green and gold!

ANC, raise up our flag!
So that it flies high;
Raise up our flag!

It has three symbols;
Every symbol
has a meaning;
The black
is the black person,
The green
our motherland,
The yellow our gold;
Raise up our flag!

– James Mothapo, Tholongwe.

Slave in my father's land

My humanity made me a slave in my father's house and my humanity made me a begging dwarf among the prosperous giants.

I remember those days before you arrived. I remember those beautiful normal days when there was peace, prosperity and harmony in my father's house.

We were generous philanthropists, an understanding and respectable family.

Now, I have a painful teardrop on my cheek because my generosity cost me a fortune and threw me into the river of poverty and oblivion.

My philanthropy misled me into believing that you were a companion, a "bra" and a friend in need and in deed.

My understanding and respect of life, culture, love and neighbourliness rendered me a target of your unscrupulous and selfish attitude.

You are ungrateful, devious and unrepenting my friend.

You call my home "Jou Vaderhuis", you stripped me of my dignity and manhood in front of children, you call me names in front of your wife and kids.

Ungibiza isiphukuphuku, umbulali, umkomonisi …

You call my dear and beloved mama by her name with no respect for her womanhood.

You call me an illiterate bum, a rascal, a rapist and unprincipled – yet you are in my father's house.

Now, bold man, tell me: "ke etse eng ka wena, he?"

Do you want me to kick you out now, or later, or do you want to negotiate?

The choice is yours my friend.

Mina ngithi, mayibuye indlu kababa!

– Jeffrey G Masemene, Kliptown.

State of Emergency in the classroom

The teacher ordered the students to write an essay on a chapter of a prescribed book which features a lot about the police and army. All the students did their work except Sipho, who forgot.

When he arrived at school the following morning he quickly wrote the introduction and a few sentences, then handed in his work.

The teacher demanded an explanation.

Sipho replied: "Due to the present state of emergency the Bureau of Information would not allow me to say any more regarding the police and security forces. The information which is in those spaces is banned."

– Sipho Abram Mokoena, Siyabuswa.

My name is Uhuru

The morning dew settled gently on the yellow vegetation on the small farming town of Interpretersfontein.

The dusty roads winding through the country-side led to the town's centre of social activity, Boetie's shabby department store.

Boetie was a fat, slightly pink man with ginger hair, who always wore a mustard safari suit. He was the chief director of social activity in Interpretersfontein.

He opened the doors of Boetie's Department Store on Monday morning at 7 am.

Ou Boetie bounced to and fro, packing and repacking his shelves, waiting anxiously for his first visitor – John "Jan" Gerwel.

"Our Jan does not feel very cheerful this morning," decided Boetie. "He must have had a hectic weekend."

"Goeie more Jan!"

"Goeie more Boetie!"

Boetie popped the big question: "How was your weekend?"

"Ag, I don't know. Those darkies staying by the bottom of my farm give me sleepless nights," replied Jan.

"They built those houses from zinc and wood and now it seems the whole Pondo tribe lives there."

Boetie assumed an academic look and pondered the next question. "Why are those darkies giving you sleepless nights, Jan?" he asked.

31

"Ag, I don't know," replied Jan.

"I think we treat our darkies very well. In our vaderland, we gave them 10 countries, like Transkei ... but they don't appreciate what we do for them."

"They got their own governments and a lot of farming land."

"Don't lie, what farms?" asked Boetie stupidly.

"Don't talk so loud. Well ... they have their own land and they should be proud of it," snapped Jan.

The door suddenly opened. Sipho had come to buy food for his family.

"Dumelang," greeted Sipho.

"Ja, Josef, what do you want?" said Boetie arrogantly.

"My naam is nie Josef nie. I want a loaf of brown bread, a pint of milk and butter," responded Sipho.

He paid for the items and left the shop, slamming the door behind him.

"You see what I mean?" exclaimed Jan.

"They don't have manners but they want to live in our vaderland and with all that nonsense about Mandela.

"Ou FW is giving them too much, you see!

"The next thing," continued Jan in an agitated voice, "they will want my farm, my two BMWs, my holiday cottage in Margate, my time-sharing village in the Drakensberg ... and my daughters."

"Old Terre'Blanche is right, we must fight and keep our vaderland white."

Suddenly there was shock in Boetie's

voice. "Look Jan, here comes Josef with the Pondo tribe, met 'kieries!!!"
"Good morning Josef," said Boetie timidly.
"My name is not Josef, you fat slob. My name is Uhuru."

– Tsholofelo Mosia, Coligny.

4. THE CURRENT VIOLENCE

The Third Force

The Third Force
moves around the township
Hunting and killing
innocent people,
destroying all their shacks,
leaving them in the cold.

The Third Force.
Everyone is in a pool of confusion,
they don't know who is to blame.
People say ANC is the killer, others say it's
PAC or Inkatha.
No! It's the Third Force.

The Third Force.
People are living in fear
because of this force.
They are so cruel
and not ashamed to attack
mourners at a night vigil.

The Third Force.
If they are arrested
– which is seldom –
they get out on bail
and their cases disappear.
They are beyond the law.

The Third Force.
Nobody can be trusted,
neither the SAP or SADF
in their terrible Hippos.

The Third Force.
When people talk of them
they say their eyes are brown.
Iph'indl' eyekhay'ezulwini,
because they don't want to face a cruel death.

– Author unknown.

Stop the killings

What is wrong with you fellow Africans?
What is it you are fighting for
When the doors of freedom
are to be opened?
For war is a pain;
an incurable pain

Please, brothers and sisters
Put your weapons down and let
us finally enjoy the fruits of our hard labour
that which we strived and
longed for many years ago
for war breaks the unity among us

What is it you are doing?
Can't you see that war
has no reward after all?
Why; because this will only
take away our good leader
please stop the killing

Let us talk matters peacefully
so as to forgive those
who wronged us
thereby making a reconciliation
for war, especially black-on-black
violence holds no future to Africans.

Is this the way maybe
of rejoicing the release
of our greatest leaders
who we awaited for many years
to come and open the doors of freedom
for us
please stop the killing

–Joseph Nkambule, Mhluzi.

Tell us …

Tell us how many people
were killed in the hostels,
were lost in Tokoza
before you tell us that troops
are in the townships
to protect us

Tell us the number
of vigilantes
who are in detention
before you tell us
that detention
is for public safety

Tell us about houses
built for the homeless
before you tell us about
the Squatter Act

Tell us about the killers of
Delekile Khoza
and Dreymond Morapedi
before you tell us about
law and order

Tell us about jobs
you have offered us
before you tell us
to pay rent

Tell us the truth …

– Julius Dhlamini, Jouberton.

Forced to kill

I've killed a man
because of hate
I thought I could forgive
but I never thought to forget
How can I forgive if I cannot forget?

I've killed a man
because of hate
I have fallen into the valley of hopelessness
A valley where love is a stranger
A valley where love is declared illegal.

I've killed a man
because of hate
Culture of blood is what I am a product of
Culture of blood is what hate is breeding
Culture of blood is the product of apartheid,
the philosophy of fear
Hate has made me fear nothing but fear.

I have a sad history to tell
A history riddled with bullets
A history full of panga-wielding men
A history of black killing black
A history of men killing one another
To secure one's political ideologies.

Is this the price I have to pay for freedom?
If 'yes' be the answer then I foresee danger
For if I concentrate only on victory
Making no compromise on my political
ideologies
I will find a germ containing another war.

My brothers and sisters
Let us stop painting the word freedom with
blood
Let us not turn our country into a wasteland
Let us have one unitary front
Let us do something!

– Sibusiso Carl Mnisi, Tembisa.

You may be next

In this land of oppression there are many murderers who continue to kill, but are never arrested.

The day before yesterday it was David Webster, yesterday it was Sicelo Dhlomo and today it was Bheki Mlangeni.

Tomorrow it might be you or me.

Chairman of the ANC's Jabulani branch, Bheki Mlangeni, was murdered by a bomb hidden in the earphones of a tape recorder sent to him as a present.

"Who killed Bheki Mlangeni?"

Was it a plan by an exiled police captain? Or was it the CCB or the Askaris? Or was it the regime?

Someone killed a talented activist and the police will again fail to 'find' the murderer.

– Richard Hlongwane, Empumalanga.

Have respect for life

How much safer we would be if everyone had a respect for life!

But many do not have such respect. Violence and bloodshed are on the increase everywhere.

A person's life is in danger if he walks in the street.

So accustomed has the world become to violence that, even for entertainment, people will sit for hours and watch it on television or at the movies.

The Bible says life is sacred.

The author of the Bible – who is also the giver of life – is the supreme authority on the subject. His laws are to be respected.

– Abram Seakamela, Alberton.

Put peace first

Day in and day out when I am looking forward to watching the news or reading the newspaper all I see or read is terror, broken hearts and sorrow.

Men are killing each other while our leaders are begging for peace.

But we people are unwilling. Is this the price we have to pay for the new South Africa?

Come on, everybody. Love your brother. Let us all stand together right now. Let us put peace first.

–Curtis Flame, Kimberley.

No life

I hate unfair
retrenchment;
When someone is hungry
he can be used;
When someone is cold
he can become violent.

When someone
is retrenched
every corner becomes a
battlefield
every street
a trench for combat,
every house
an army base.

Why privatisation,
Which means
unfair retrenchment
and more violence?
Only blacks are hard hit
by Mr Hunger.

Most members of the
black working class
cannot afford
to live
because of
unfair retrenchment.

–Martins Sebaka, Evaton.

Unemployment dehumanises

He wakes up in the morning
Thinking of what he is going to do that day,
But not much is in store for him
He doesn't like the situation he is in.
He asks why him?
He buys a newspaper and sees a vacancy
So he calls
But they tell him the job has been filled.
Next day he buys the paper again
And runs to phone,
But still no luck.
He decides to go door to door.
When he enters the premises
The big "No Vacancy" sign greets him,
But he ignores it and goes right in.
The white lady at reception
Without even looking at him says,
"There's no vacancy!"
He tries to explain,
But she's too busy to talk.
Why is the world so unfair?
He goes home dejected
His stomach asks him a frightening question
"When last did you feed me?"
He searches his pockets to buy something
But the remaining coins can only get him
home.
As a man, he'll persevere.
He asks himself if there is anyone who can
save him.
The answer is a mystery

At times he wished it were just a bad dream,
But it is a living reality
He has to face.

– Author unknown.

Job hunt a real struggle

How hard and miserable
to be educated
and still have to wander
from office to office
struggling to look for a job.

Applying in writing
and regret is the answer.
Respond to a newspaper
advert – they want experience.
Which comes first,
the job or experience?

Personal attempts
are met by clerks
who tell you
they don't have vacancies.
They insist you
see the manager
or threaten to call security.

When will apartheid stop
and equal work opportunities
be generated?

– GO Motsage, Kimberley.

Good morning South Africa!

I wonder when it will
come –
When one will wake up
from a deep sleep
and be greeted by a voice
from the radio saying
"Good morning
South Africa!
The day of freedom has come"

In church priests will kneel
chanting prayers of freedom
"Free at last. Free at last.
"Thank God. We are free!"

Workers join hands
singing one song –
of the end of exploitation
that will unite all workers.
"Thank God we are free!"

In parliament
the new president will speak
From apartheid
to people's power
From exile to freedom
Freedom in our lifetime
Yes, we are free at last
Good morning new nation!

– Richard Shilenge, Kabokweni.

Victims of a backlash

Saying that this is the beginning of
white resistance
They also realise that now is the end
Of white domination and exploitation
They come tottering into the township of
Thabong
Making repeated attacks on our brothers
and sisters.

Hardened by fear
Weakened by mistrust over the tyrant
government
And tested by bitterness born of violence
They rampage every "darkie" they come
across in the night
EINA! Askies my baas
It is not me
The wind of change is blowing
Over the land south of the Limpopo.

Uhuru is always better organised than the
Apart-hate and tyranny
Who shall stand guard to the guards
themselves?
Comrades and compatriots, the time has
come
To join hands

Unity is stronger than thunder
The last mile of the journey
Is probably the longest and hardest
Just leave room for hope and healing
Because history
Is busy judging the ENEMY.

– George Mokoena, Bethlehem

Freedom at last

Yes I can hear the drums beating
And I can tell from the sounds coming
That we will no longer be weeping
That soon we will be celebrating
Our freedom from bondage

Yes I can see high up the sky
The glittering little stars that are shy
And here I stand and embrace
The moon the moment it descends
On the blessed soil of mother Africa

I can hear in Africa songs of freedom
I can tell using my poetic wisdom
In the South we'll be writing history
Wielding high our spear of victory

Yes I can see at dawn the smiling sun
Blinding my eyes with powerful rays
That give warmth irrespective of race

Come freedom, let your waters flow
like a stream
In the south you're
a long-cherished dream
Come and quench our hunger
and thirst
And nurture to full bloom
the tree of liberty
Come freedom, we've long been waiting.

– Joseph Nkambule, Mhluzi.

Racism still alive and well

I've spoken to the damaged children
heard the endless tales of woe
seen the guns, knives and bodies
of the last decade

I've watched the rulers
move even further away from
offering the basic
requirements of human life –
work, family, safety, the law.

The black underclass is the cause,
says the white man
There are continuing reports of whites
using force to keep the blacks from
moving into their neighbourhoods.
White policemen are too quick to arrest
or lock up black suspects.

Racism continues to be real in South Africa
Only a fool will deny it.

– Thekwini Ncongwane, Ermelo.

Mr Freedom

He went to prepare a paradise for us all.
He went away, but not to stay.
Soon, very soon I shall sing freedom songs.
When the trumpet of freedom sounds
Oppression and iron bars shall open.

He is coming back, our true leader.
He will free us from the chains of slavery.
He is coming to free us from ideology.
This man will hold freedom words,
Let the handsome son of mother soil free us.

Mr Freedom is coming to free us all.
We are in need of equal rights, no colour bias.
Terrorism Act, Group Areas Act must go,
Bannings and harassment must go.

Give us our beautiful Azania.

Our soul and spirit is crying for our son.
We are crying for the convicted oppressed.
When he comes there will be no more pain.

– Ronnie Nemungadi, Sibasa.

A decade of change

This was the decade
that saw the cultural boycott.
That saw Samora Machel killed under
strange circumstances.
That saw the iron lady who opposed sanctions
step down after almost a decade of power.
That saw coloureds, Indians, Mangope and
Sebe
opting for the system.
The decade that experience bombs, limpet
mines,
AK 47s and terror tactics.
That was tired of blood staining the land;
the blood our youth shed in the name of
liberation.
The decade that saw the invention of the
necklace.
An inquest into the death of David Webster
in vain.
That survived a State of Emergency,
detention, death
sentences, life sentences.
And ultimately the decade that brought the
release of
comrade Mandela from jail.

– RBM Siele, Pretoria.

Boereseun changed his mind

He is a white man
a real boereseun
with an Afrikaner
upbringing.
He went to the army
and enjoys rugby
like most Afrikaners.

My skin is black
his is white
My eyes are brown
his are blue,
a true blue Afrikaner.

He's a law graduate
now works in the courts.
But what's wrong
with this boereseun
who has rebelled
against his volk?

He hates unjust laws
He hates the colour bar
He's been suffering
that's why
he's changed
his mind to
fight for equal rights
He's a real kafferboetie.

– Leonard Maifala, Majaneng

The pain of going into exile

Dear South Africa

It has been a long,
lonely and painful time
since I and you parted
during the bitter days of
apartheid

Ever since I left you,
I've been wandering the
world over trying to find
someone to replace you.

But nowhere could I find
someone suitable to fill
the empty space inside
my heart
which eagerly awaits your
tender, loving arms.

I'm still battling
against all odds
to keep our vow –
until death do us part.

Hoping to come
back home
as soon as possible.

Yours in struggle,
exiled child of the soil.

–Joseph Nkambule, Mhluzi.

Motherland welcome your son

Tears of misery were your food while your
son was away.
Oh! Motherland your son is back.
Oh! South Africa rejoice with the whole
world.
Stand up and with both hands welcome your
son.

Let tears of joy fill your eyes.
Oh! South Africa your son loves you.
He loves you more than his own life.
Oh! Motherland welcome your son.

Oh! Motherland your son is a hero.
The whole world knows him.
He was jailed for 27 years because of his
motherland.
Oh! Motherland welcome him with tears of
joy.

South Africa stand up and sing and dance.
Your son has returned safe.
Oh! Motherland welcome your son.

– Reckson Makunga, Melville.

Education is the weapon

Education is like
a big tree
That is planted in good soil.
Its leaves are green,
its fruits are ripe,
its shade is cool.

It's the only way to success.
It's the pillar of society
and the structure, though
the road to victory is tough.

We must not allow fear
to rule our lives.
Hiding from our problems
will never make us men.
We must take our weapons
and arm ourselves
for a better future.
Education is the weapon.

We are a stream which is part
of a big river
Flowing in the direction
of progress.
We need an education.
Our future depends
on our achievements.
Let's arm ourselves
for a new bright South Africa.

– T Jele, Embalenhle.

Man must read

Reading is the art of the mind.
Like the stomach,
The mind becomes hungry for knowledge.
Food is the remedy for physical hunger
Reading is the remedy for mental hunger.

To stay in good health, man must eat
To make the mind think clearly and quickly,
Man must read.
Like an athlete who practises every day
The mind also needs practice.

To read everyday is to acquire more
knowledge
To acquire more knowledge is to feed the
mind
and to feed the mind is to develop skills.

– Carlo Matabane, Argyle.

No answer to my plea

I thought it was clear
when I said
"Away with Bantu Education!"
I thought it was clear enough.
When I continued to protest
amid your torture,
you turned a deaf ear.

Your answer was my brother's death
Your answer was brother's gagging
My disability cannot be compensated
by high fences around schools.
You made my teacher quit,
leaving me in the wilderness.
Can he be replaced by a soldier
from the border?
I thought it was clear enough then.
If it wasn't, it should be by now.

– Harrison Motlhari, Kagiso.

Gone are the days

Gone are the days
when we used to play hide and seek.
I still yearn for them.
The days we used to respect our teachers,
and we differentiated between
adults and youngsters.

I remember the days when
teachers were lords of our townships.
No one was allowed to drink.
No one was allowed to smoke.
No one was allowed to be absent.
No one was allowed to fall in love.
Nowadays our certificates
are as worthless as toilet paper.

– E Nyerenda, Thembisa.

Examination

For a long long time
He gazes steadfastly at the question paper
He held in trembling hands.
None of the questions could he tackle,
His answer sheet was still blank.
He sighed in shock and despair.
Suddenly a loud voice pierced the still hall –
"Pens down!"

– David Hlatshwayo, Mpuluzi.

Learning bears success

The wise and great have
recommended education
as the magic formula
for achieving success
and a comfortable life
Life without you is empty

Your roots might be sour
but your fruits are sweet
like those of a peach tree
Life without you is bitter

You are our life-blood
Life without you is hard
you are our daily bread
Without you
we suffer hunger
You are the nation's light
Life without you
is darkness

You are the magic key
Life without you means
closed doors
and less employment
You are to us
the spear of the nation
Our future without you means death.

– Joseph Nkambule, Mhluzi.

The folly of a dropout

Alfred was a 15-year-old boy who disliked school.

He came from a wealthy family and though his parents tried to encourage him to love school, he could not.

So Alfred dropped out of school even before he had learnt to read or write.

He felt that because his parents were wealthy he would never have to struggle to make a living for himself.

So why should he bother with an education, he thought?

Some years later, his parents died – and as he expected, he inherited all their money.

But all those working in his business knew he could not read or write and his cousin was responsible for signing all important papers.

Alfred trusted his cousin, forgetting that one should not trust a stone.

One day his cousin made a plan to gain control of all Alfred's money.

Alfred even put his mark on the papers, but could not read that he was signing his wealth away.

So Alfred's property went to his cousin and all he was left with was the clothes on his back.

He became a begger and could not even find work.

He began to see the importance of education.

– Gerald Mzizi, Tumahole.

The Zoo

Children from my school went to visit the zoo last month.

It was the first time I ever saw a lion. I have read that lions are very fierce when they live in the bush, but these lions looked very sleepy.

We also saw a hippopotamus who looked like he would like a big river to swim in, not a small dam. He was very shy and refused to come up from under the water to show his face to all the children staring at him. We only saw bubbles when he came up for air.

The animals I did not like were the snakes. There was one big, fat one with dark spots that was curled up in the corner. It looked like those snakes that squeeze you to death before eating you.

We had a nice picnic under the trees, with ice cream and chips.

– Tumelo Leballo, Alexandra Township.

Hint for a better quality education

The standard of education in South Africa is very low compared to other countries. Many things can be done to improve our education.

Firstly, every school must have a laboratory and a library.

The laboratory must be well equipped so students can carry out their own experiments. The library must have many books and teachers must encourage students to use them.

Secondly, in South Africa most black students are unable to express themselves in English, so students must speak English at school because it is the major language of South Africa.

Thirdly, students must be able to watch videos at school because this is one way of teaching, and students do not easily forget what they see.

Finally, students are taught about places they have never seen, so they must go on tours to see such places.

–Zakhele Ntshangase, Colenso.

Dearest Mama

Dearest Mama, I'll always remember you
When I am happy or sad
For you are the kindest, dearest mother in the
world.

I remember the days
When I had no money for school
And when I went without food
Yet you tried hard to keep me in school.

My younger brothers cried to you
"Mother we are hungry!"
And you embraced them and comforted
them
With your sweet voice.

In the cold of winter you were the first to rise
To go to work
In the rain, the wind
You were always off on the road to work.

On Mother! You are the bravest woman in the
world.
There were times when you were ill,
When you could not walk or talk
But you never gave up.

I'll always remember your encouraging
words:
"Be bold and brave my son,
"For this world has thorns that prick hard.

"It needs a courageous man to defeat it.
"So don't lose hope and you'll be a man."

Mama! I'll never forget you
For you brought light to my world.

– Mkhethwa Shongwe, KaNyamazane.

Grandmother

I love my grandmother with all my heart
She is an ancient girl, her pace has changed,
of course
My grandmother of ninety is my love
She is a teller of tales
She is old, old and always cold
Indeed she is never far from a fireplace
"Makadzoka" she is called, for she once died
After some time she rose from death
"Mushakabvudimbu" they call her in Shona
– half dead
My life is in her hands and the life of my
family too
She is half witch, having been taught to cure
with herbs
Her eyes are half out but the sense of touch is
strong
The sense of smell is there for she can smell
herbs
Little thin grandmother of mine!
Looking so young because of eating so many
sweets
Sugar-sucker! Ten spoons in each cup of tea
My old amabuya! Makadzoka is my goddess
She hates dirt, noisy quarrels and dry food
She is ever sitting on her mat in the sun
otherwise hunting for herbs
She is ever smiling, but an egg grows in her
throat
When one annoys her
"I wish to die and rest," she says

"When will this world end?"
"I am tired"
Beside her is a packet of sugar, a sauce of
peppered corn
Her teeth are brown with rust, her nose sooty
with black snuff
Makadzoke is my love
I shall look into her dimples
The laughing dimples are on her chin
There were two, but there are now a hundred
There are holes where stagnant water
Was scooped out
Lovely Mashakabvu
My grandmother is my love.

– Mavis Seema, Kwa-Xuma, Soweto.

Thief

Thief, you don't sleep
You are always moving around the town
Searching for money
Stealing cars
Why can't you buy your own?
You always rob our parents.

When they come back home
You wait for them at the corners of streets
holding knives and guns.
You even write letters to our parents
telling them they must pay
money for protection

– Vincent Aphane, Temba.

The glue, the child and the night-mare

I am a victim of poverty
I live by begging
Odd jobs and thievery
I am a streetchild

As the winter wind whips
Through suburbs and city
I can be seen huddled
In a shop's doorway
A piece of cardboard
Over my body
Taking a sniff from my glue bottle
Hoping to block out the cold
Hoping to sleep

I doze fitfully
Through the long night
In the morning
I wake, not with joy
And hope for a new day
But with pains of hunger and cold
With the desperate need to survive
For I am an outcast from society
My crime is having no home
No parents, no place to sleep
I'm a child of the streets . . . .

I can be seen at many an intersection
Or car park
Alone
Or in groups
Begging, finding parking, pilfering
Picking pockets, shoplifting

At night I sleep in gutters
Dustbins, drainpipes, doorways
Graveyards, parks and scrapyards
Deserted buildings and old cars
Sometimes I build a fire
And often dreadful burns result
From dozing too close to the flames
And I'm affected by disease
I cannot escape
My constant misery, my glue
I'm a streetchild

Different people
From different places
Knew me by different names
Cape Town calls me stroller
Johannesburg and Durban
Know me as streetchild
Or malunde or malalapipe
I'm twilight child and skadukind
But whatever they call me
I present a pitiful problem
That they must not ignore
I'm a streetchild.

– Simon Mosolotsane, Carletonville.

A plea from a Twilight Child

Why turn blind eyes on me
For I am not an animal
But just a twilight child, a tramp
I have no place to sleep
No-one cares for me
Look at my weather-beaten face
My clothes are as old as mountains
and they smell like rotten eggs
But why turn blind eyes on me

I stay nowhere and sleep all over
The city knows me well
When the day breaks it excites me not
For there is nothing new in it
When the night comes
Tears begin to fall on my lizard-skin face
Because of the cold I suffer
Why turn blind eyes on me

I have tried to reform in vain
Whenever I try to join society
It looks down on me,
Spits on me heavily
Calling me hurtful names
Dustbins provide fresh and rotten food
But why turn blind eyes on me

My soul is alive
It want spiritual fulfilment
But where can it get it from
For my face tells it all

Dear Lord, please be on my side
Remember me on judgement day
Keep me on your right-hand side
Forgive all the sins I have committed
But why turn blind eyes on me

– Benedict Khumalo, Orlando West.

Where are my parents?

My father and mother got divorced when I was a very young child. My mother went away without saying a word to me and so did my father.

When I saw my parents leaving, I waved goodbye, thinking they would be back soon. I thought Daddy and Mama would come back to their only son. But they didn't and my uncle took care of me.

Now my schooling is over and I am entering a new phase of life. Again I have to adjust to whatever circumstances I come across. I am an orphan and got to where I am through the charity of my uncle.

Where are my parents?

– Joshua Moroenyane, Phomolong, Kroonstad.

My mother left me 10 days after I was born and I have not seen her since.

I also know nothing of my father.

I believe my mother is married to another man and has a family. How I wish I could see them and love them – but it is only wishful thinking.

Often I cry myself to sleep thinking about my parents.

I was brought up by a white lady who took me from my mother when she rejected me. This lady loves me and I care about her a lot.

She is my mother and my father and she says I must never leave her.

She is now quite old.

I wonder why she sacrificed her life to be a mother to me.

But something is missing – that feeling of being able to say "mother" or "father".

I wish I was near my own parents. Why don't they look me up? Why, they don't care for me.

– Zakhele Hadebe, Steadville.

The homeless need care

My heart bleeds when I think about the plight of the homeless, especially at this cold time of the year.

Dragging their tattered and torn blankets in the heart of the "Golden City", they do not have even a cent to buy hot soup to ward off the chill.

Every time I buy a newspaper I read about programmes being set up to cater for these unfortunate souls, but whenever I go into town more of them are gathered in parks and on pavements drinking, sniffing glue or quarrelling.

Often I put my hand into my pocket to give them some money for food. But I don't feel I've done enough.

Much has to be done for these victims of poverty and broken homes.

Rehabilitation centres should be set up for them. Society should provide for them.

– Edwin Tsietsi Mahange.

A boy who persevered

A 15-year-old boy whose parents died when he was 10 was living with his aunt and was in Std 7 at school.

But his aunt treated him badly and he remembered his father telling him: "To get what you want you have to fight for it", so he ran away and went looking for a job.

He first went into the house of a wealthy family who asked him whether he had done garden work before. He said "no", but he would do all he could. They said they did not need chancers.

The following morning he went to another house where they asked him if he could ride a bicycle. He said he could, although he could not. Every morning they sent him to the dairy. On a bicycle it took 10 minutes. This boy also took 10 minutes, but he ran with the bicycle because he could not ride it.

His employer was not aware of this because of the short time the boy took.

After a year, a neighbour saw him running with the bicycle and asked his employer why he treated the boy so badly.

Next morning they followed the boy and saw him running at an unbelievable speed with the bicycle.

They asked him why he said he could ride a bicycle when he could not. He said he thought they were not going to give him the job, and he cried.

They felt very sorry for him and decided to send him back to school because they saw that he was prepared to achieve something in life.

Today he is a doctor through hard work and determination. He always remembered his father's saying: "To get what you want you have to fight for it."

– Meshack Madonsela, Harrismith

Celebrating our Mama Africa

God, in his wisdom, created
Miriam, who could make the heart sing
Who'd be a delight to her nation.
He made her a bright combination
Of charm and of a songbird proud
of its culture and roots.
A picture of natural intelligence
With so many inspiring traditional
songs to utter.
Her smile as warm as sunshine above.
He looked at the heavens around him.
And gave her an angel's beauty.
God finished his lovely creation
And sent her to earth so she'd be
Part of a nation who'd cherish
And treasure a real African mother.

– Tshidiso Motale, Maokeng.

* Miriam Makeba is fondly known as "Mama
Africa"

Praise 'King Didiza'

He's handsome, but
is hated by some
for the mess he does to them.

Speed is his asset,
being hurt is
his concern.
Pacing is his talent
which makes
defenders lament.

He circles them all,
he lets them fall.
Goals are his game.
He cannot be tamed.

Who is he?
This ball wizard,
who, whenever he's in
possession of the ball,
sends a chill down
opposition coaches'
spines?

He is no newcomer
to the game.
It's Fanie Madida,
"Didiza" to
his admirers.
The Phefeni boy
is a speedy winger
who is a marvel to watch.

– Michael Jaca, Peddie

* Fanie Madida is a famous soccer player

Soccer

We come from Soweto, from south of the
border,
and west of the sunshine, a township for
workers.

It's where we play soccer, the game of the
people;
more flowing than rugby, much faster than
cricket.

We pass with the right foot and shoot with
the left foot,
control with a knee-bounce and head from a
corner.

On waste-ground and playgrounds with
stones for the goalposts.
At cafes and garages, shops and street-
corners,
We practice our flick-kicks and think of our
starlets.

The Chiefs and the Swallows, the Bucs and
Black Aces.
Birds, Chiefs or Swallows, they're all our
game's heroes.

Forget for the moment our schoolbooks and
teachers,
we're fanatical sportsmen and footballing
creatures.

Now we're marching in thousands on
Orlando Stadium
to see the Cup Final, with whistles and
banners
to cheer on the winner.

Ask us what is a computer? It's a man-made
machine.
Is there one in Soweto? Yes! Computer
Lamola.

And what is a teenager? A young man of
school age
in jeans and a T-shirt? No! Our Teenage
Dladla.

But the greatest of all is Jomo E Sono,
the wizard of dribble who left us to travel
across the Atlantic.

So applause for the players both losers and
winners.
One day we'll be experts though now we're
beginners!

– Benjamin Radebe, Motsethabong.

Saturday in the township

People moving
up and down
Others sitting on the lawn
The day for shopping
Car-hooters shouting
Everyone likes this day
Because they're away – to
a picnic, maybe

Stokvels, here
And there
Saturday, a day of
Various performances
Others making changes
The whole township
Filled with excitement
And friendship dominant

No school
On to the swimming pool
For summer has already
commenced

"Happy birthday to you
You're now two"
I heard a voice
In the next house
Yeah! Saturday
Has a good atmosphere.

– Isaac Tshepo, Mokgatle.

Phola Park blues

Thokoza, Thokoza
People packed like sardines
in matchbox houses
Phola Park
What have we done to you?

Fathers running for trains
but they get so little back
Children eager to learn
but they get teargassed or shot

Come Sunday, everyone's home
Girls in Shebeens drink like men
Mothers cry softly and
their tears flow
like water in the sea
Thokoza, there's no easy road to freedom.

—Vusumzi Tshabalala, Thokoza.

The shackdwellers

Our fellows are suffering
Suffering from colds
Sleeping in unfinished shacks.

Moving up and down
Transporting heavy goods
Carrying buckets of water
Latrines are unavailable.

People shouting
Shouting for delivery of zincs
Others shouting for help of their seniors

Looking around for lost properties
Thin dogs wandering
Through dirt and litter.

They have built shacks very deep
Deep in the bush
Forgotten about snakes, noisy rats,
tarantulas ...
Insects will degenerate
Diseases will abound
Oh! Shackdwellers, what a great suffering.

– Irvin Molelekoa, Jouberton Location.

Pulsating Sebokeng

At a glance, Sebokeng looks dull and lifeless. Almost all the houses are built to the same pattern – thousands upon thousands of small matchbox houses separated from each other by wire fencing.

Yet there are few places I know which are as lively as this enormous township.

There are people, no doubt, who grumble that Sebokeng is too far from town and the factories where everybody works – and that many of the houses are still without electricity although Africa's biggest power station is next door.

Yet, in spite of this, Sebokeng lives. It lives insecurely, sometimes dangerously, but with a determined will to survive.

Not many people earn much money here. There are thousands who don't eat three meals a day. There are homes where husbands give instructions that visitors are not to be served with tea, however long they may stay. That is the more depressing face of this place.

But then Sebokeng has many faces. For instance, the number of large American cars never fails to amaze outsiders. There are streets where every other house has a car in the yard.

Admittedly, some of them don't go, but they are there all the same.

The man of the house is able to say: "You can't miss my house, there is a black Chev in the yard" – even if the poor thing has been on bricks for years.

This is the way of things in Sebokeng. A pattern of uneventful, economical living, occasionally interrupted by great moments. It may be one unforgettable night, one extravagant weekend, or the good living may last a whole year.

You see this at the drinking parties.

A man will take his whole week's pay and buy drinks for half a dozen of his friends. "Fill the table and count the empties," he will say to the shebeen queen. The idea seems to be to live well while you can and face the troubles of tomorrow when they come.

There are other people whose "moments of life" come in a different way.

The girls, for example, who begin to live when they get into their Sunday best and go to weddings. Others will spend much of their pay on a black shawl to be worn at an important funeral at the weekend.

All the time the pattern is the same, people live erratically, in snatches of a life they can never afford to lead for long in Sebokeng.

– Thabeki Mbele, Sebokeng.

Roger came to stay in our location after living on a farm where he had spent his entire life.

In fact Roger had never spent time in a town and had only come to town because he had a quarrel with the farmer over some cows.

Soon after he arrived, he went to look for a job.

He stood at the side of the road waiting for a taxi. He had never taken a taxi before, so he was not sure what to do.

A big truck came zooming past and Roger threw his hat into the air, shouting, "Taxi wait! I'm going to town!"

Other people waiting for the taxi laughed at him and when the taxi arrived, showed him what to do.

Inside the taxi, he sat in the front seat next to the driver and adjusted the rear-view mirror so that he could look at himself. Puzzled, the driver asked him what he was doing.

"I want to see that I'm sitting inside a taxi," Roger replied.

His surprise was even greater when the taxi arrived in town and he saw the big buildings, cars, and traffic lights.

In his awe at the speed and size of the town, Roger nearly got run over, but managed to crawl onto the pavement where he praised God for saving his life. Passers-by laughed at the poor man.

He decided to go home, where he told his sorry tale to his wife, who sagely replied: "You live and learn."

– Ishamael Nkosana Ngozo, Bethlehem.

Selling shoes to shackdwellers

I had to go selling house to house; "R20. Ayashisa amateki!"

One lady said: "Ag shame lovey, I have just bought mala le mogudu for supper."

I had to go house to house again. Most houses had tin shacks in their backyards.

Where do they come from? I asked myself. Ciskei, Transkei and Cape Town. Why? They speak Xhosa and this is a Tswana township.

"Molweni Bosisi ayashisa amateki R20!"

"Oh siyaxolisa. Asinamali!" (Forgive us, we have no money).

But one decided to buy a pair. Three more followed.

"One buys, we all buy. She is not the only one who can afford tackies."

I thought about these people, the shacks they live in, those broken windows.

What will they do?

Don't worry. They aren't black like the night, or brown like sand. They are beautiful.

– Faith Rabotapi, Orlando West.

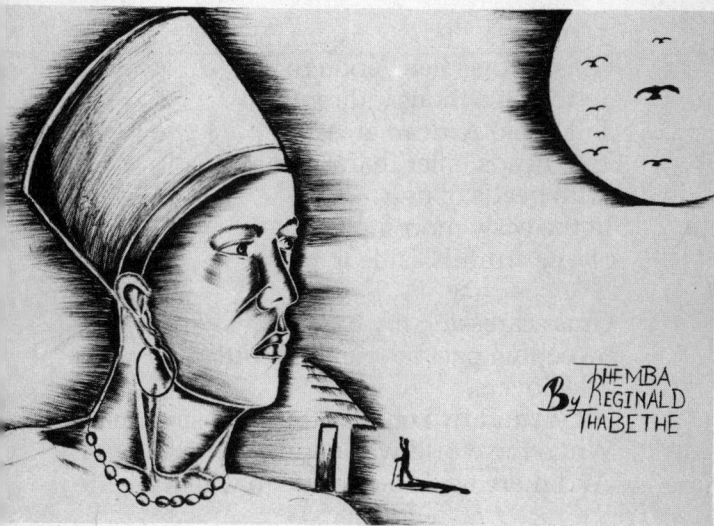

By Themba Reginald Thabethe

Tall khaki African grass

Grass grows here, enough
To thatch a thousand roofs
Tall khaki African grass
Two heads taller than I, laden
With beads of dew.
In the early morning I
Shove armfuls aside to pass.

Grass caressing my bare thighs
Sweeping past me rustling softly
Like lovers.
Adam and Eve once in this wild savannah
When the world was young
And there was no-one else to watch.

It's hard to think that this tall crop
Coarse in its maturity
Burst out of its October black burnt plains
Green and succulent, and savouring the
mellow sun
Grew to this height.
But it's harder yet to think
That this crop will crumple
To veld fire ashes
Fruitless growth!

– Author unknown.

Mother Africa

Oh, our mother Africa
Our mother country
You are the only mother
We rely on you.

Oh, our mother
You provide your children
With everything they need
They depend on you.

Oh, our mother
Our beautiful mother
You gave life to us
You have all the natural resources
We need to survive
Lead and protect us
We are alive
Because of your existence.

God! We beg you
To give life
To our only mother
AFRICA.

– A poem by Sonto.

Full of harmony but no rest

Oh! Lord, what a continent,
Full of harmony but no rest
When are we going to be free,
From this colonial rule all over our land

In hundreds, thousands, they slaughter us
Oh! Africa, we are dying for you.
Where is my spear and shield to defend
myself
Our weapons have turned against us and we
are killing each other.
They are using modern equipment and we
are now clever,
I tell you comrades, this equipment will one
day free us.

–Albert Ntlonti, Kwa-Xuma.

A seed from the Great Fish River

Umpondomise kaNgxabane
Is a seed
Spouting
From the
Great Fish River

Floating
Towards
The battlefield
Of our liberation

Calling all
African bards
To sing with him

A long
Melancholy song
That draws
The powerful winds

From the deep
Oceans of
Our eternal
Place.

–BW Kwenene, Estadeal, Port Elizabeth.

Shame Africa

You're shamefaced before your sons and
daughters
once covered by a beautiful green shawl.
You were the land of promise
but wars and destruction have made you
shabby,
shattered you into pieces.
You could accommodate them all
but they turned you into a shantytown.
I shiver when I think of it, for I wouldn't
tolerate such torment. Shame Africa!

– Mongezi Nkonzombi, Mdantsane.

Come back my Africa

During the night some foreign men came
And stole your heart away from me
So lonely and poor they let me be
A shameful begger in my own land
Come back, my dear, come back.

They jailed my brother and made him toil
They shot my leader and made him boil
They raped my children and made me cry
They did almost everything to make us die
Come back to me, my dear, come back to me.

You are mine, my dear, you are mine
And nobody else but me alone
So please, my dear, so please
Come back to where you belong.

–Joseph Nkambule, Mhluzi.

A prince returns ceremoniously

Qubeka was a young prince whose father, King Dumsa, was a powerful but fair ruler.

One morning after Qubeka's 19th birthday, his father called him and said: "You will soon become king of this tribe.

"You have not even seen or toured around this beautiful country and you have not even met the other neighbouring tribes and their chiefs."

So the Prince set forth and for many days and nights he walked and slept under the African sky.

He met many different kinds of tribes and also introduced himself to many peaceful kings.

When Qubeka approached the well-known Lunga tribe, he was welcomed by the beautiful Princess Lundi.

For many months he stayed with the Lunga tribe, and he and Lundi grew more and more fond of each other.

One morning the King of the Lunga tribe allowed Prince Qubeka and Princess Lundi to marry.

After the celebration Qubeka took his beautiful bride back to his village.

They were met by many excited people.

King Dumsa was so proud of his son that he allowed him to rule his kingdom.

– Simphiwe Piliso, Glenashley, Durban.

The war that never was

In the olden days the Zulus and the Basotho hated each other. One day this hatred led them to a war which they never fought.

It began like this.

The Zulu king ordered his army to attack the Basotho and teach them a lesson.

The Basotho chief did the same thing at the same time.

The Zulu army left home armed with spears made of sugar-cane. Remember sugar-cane is found all over Natal.

And the Basotho army was used to hurling stones at their enemy while they were riding on horseback. So they left for Natal on horses.

These two nations lived very far from each other and on the way the soldiers of the two armies felt hungry.

The Zulu army ate the sugar-cane and the Basotho army ate their horses.

Suddenly they came across each other and met face to face.

The Zulu leader commanded his army to fight with their bare hands, but the warriors protested, saying they could not fight without weapons.

And the Basotho army told their commander they could not fight without their horses.

So the two mighty armies were forced to retreat without having struck a single blow.

– Gerald Mzizi, Tumahole.

Smargha

Humanity fails but God reigns

When I imagine the future,
I find my mind filled with fear.
There's a big question gnawing at
my nerves, like an ulcer
that corrodes the stomach.
What will this world be
like in ten year's time?
Humanity is threatened
by a nuclear explosion,
wars, and famine.
But in spite of all this,
I find solace in the knowledge that
God is still on the throne.
If we look back we would find
that the times we
failed were when we
substituted man's will
for God's will.

– David Ntho Mashakwe-Tswai, Koringpunt.